Spreading Kindness

Being Kind to Friends

by Brienna Rossiter

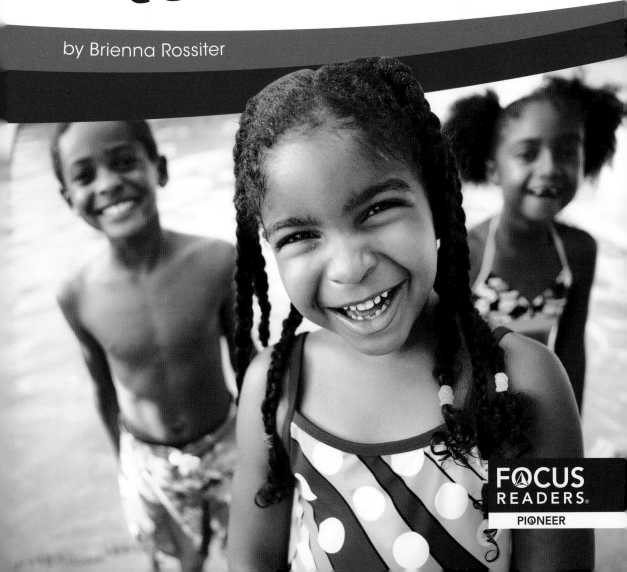

FOCUS
READERS.

PIONEER

www.focusreaders.com

Focus Readers is distributed by North Star Editions:
sales@northstareditions.com | 888-417-0195

Produced for Focus Readers by Red Line Editorial.

Photographs ©: iStockphoto, cover, 1, 16; Shutterstock Images, 4, 7, 8, 10, 13, 14, 18, 20

Library of Congress Cataloging-in-Publication Data
Names: Rossiter, Brienna, author.
Title: Being kind to friends / by Brienna Rossiter.
Description: Lake Elmo, MN : Focus Readers, [2021] | Series: Spreading
   kindness | Includes index. | Audience: Grades 2-3
Identifiers: LCCN 2020036709 (print) | LCCN 2020036710 (ebook) | ISBN
   9781644936825 (hardcover) | ISBN 9781644937181 (paperback) | ISBN
   9781644937907 (pdf) | ISBN 9781644937549 (ebook)
Subjects: LCSH: Kindness--Juvenile literature. | Interpersonal
   relations--Juvenile literature. | Friends--Juvenile literature.
Classification: LCC BJ1533.K5 R67 2021 (print) | LCC BJ1533.K5 (ebook) |
   DDC 177/.7--dc23
LC record available at https://lccn.loc.gov/2020036709
LC ebook record available at https://lccn.loc.gov/2020036710

Printed in the United States of America
Mankato, MN
012021

About the Author

Brienna Rossiter is a writer and editor who lives in Minnesota. She loves cooking food and being outside.

Table of Contents

Chapter 1

A Good Friend

Friends have fun together. They also help and **encourage** one another. Good friends think of how others feel. They act in ways that show these feelings are important.

Use kind words when talking to friends. Be careful when you joke or **tease**. When you tease, make sure your friend thinks it's funny, too. And always stop if your friend asks you to.

Being a Friend

Dependable: Friends can be trusted.

Generous: Friends share.

Honest: Friends tell the truth.

Loyal: Friends stay with you.

Chapter 2

Show You Care

There are many ways to show friends you care about them. **Greet** them and use their names. Watch them **perform** or play sports. Cheer for them and their team.

If your friend is sad or in trouble, help out. Sometimes you can help solve the problem. Other times, you can help by listening to your friend talk.

Fun Fact

Good friends stand up for each other. Speak up if other people are being mean to your friend.

Encouraging Words

Words are a great way to show people you care. Think about some of your friends. What do you like about each person? What does he or she do well? Tell each friend what you thought of. You'll help your friends feel cared for.

Chapter 3

Be Fair

You can be kind to friends by treating them fairly. Share toys and games. Also, take turns when choosing what to do. It's not fair if you decide all the time.

Remember to take turns speaking. Don't **interrupt**, and don't do all the talking. Try not to **brag**. And don't talk about yourself too much. Instead, give your friends time to talk.

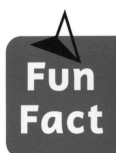

Fun Fact

A good conversation goes back and forth, like tossing a ball.

Chapter 4

Choose to Forgive

Even good friends make mistakes. They may hurt one another's feelings. But good friends also choose to **forgive** one another.

If you hurt someone, say you are sorry. If a friend hurts you, don't stay mad. Instead, talk about it. Explain how the friend made you feel. By working things out, friends show they care about each other's feelings.

Being Kind to Friends

Write your answers on a separate piece of paper.

1. Write a sentence describing one way to treat friends fairly.

2. Do you think it is harder to say you're sorry or to forgive others? Why?

3. What is a good way to talk to friends?
   - A. take turns speaking
   - B. brag about yourself
   - C. interrupt them

4. How does apologizing to friends show kindness?
   - A. It shows that they were wrong.
   - B. It shows that you don't want to hurt their feelings.
   - C. It shows that you can't change your mind.

Answer key on page 24.

Glossary

brag
To talk proudly about yourself.

encourage
To give help or support.

forgive
To let go of your anger toward someone.

greet
To say hello.

interrupt
To start talking while someone else is still talking.

perform
To act, sing, or play in front of a group.

tease
To make fun of someone. Sometimes teasing can be playful, but sometimes it can be mean.

To Learn More

BOOKS

Merk, T. M. *Painting a Peaceful Picture: Respecting Peers.* Mankato, MN: The Child's World, 2018.

Plattner, Josh. *Manners with Friends.* Minneapolis: Abdo Publishing, 2016.

NOTE TO EDUCATORS

Visit **www.focusreaders.com** to find lesson plans, activities, links, and other resources related to this title.

Index

Answer Key: 1. Answers will vary; **2.** Answers will vary; **3.** A; **4.** B